LINDA GOODMAN'S

GEMINI

LINDA GOODMAN'S SUN SIGNS

GEMINI
22 May to 21 June

Pan Books

London, Sydney and Auckland

First published in Great Britain 1970 by
George G. Harrap & Co Ltd
as part of a volume containing all twelve Sun signs
This edition published 1989 by Pan Books Ltd,
Cavaye Place, London SW10 9PG

10 9 8 7 6 5 4 3 2 1

© Linda Goodman 1968, 1989

ISBN 0 330 31002 x

Phototypeset by Input Typesetting Ltd, London
Printed and bound in Great Britain by
Richard Clay Ltd, Bungay, Suffolk

For Mike Todd
the Gemini
who really knew the people he knew
and for Melissa Anne
the Pisces
to keep a promise . . .
Thus grew the tale of Wonderland:
Thus slowly, one by one,
Its quaint events were hammered out —
And now the tale is done . . .

Acknowledgement

I would like to express my grateful thanks for the help and advice given me by my friend and teacher, astrologer Lloyd Cope, a Virgo. Without his encouragement and faith, these books might have remained just another Aries dream.

The verses used throughout the text have been taken from the works of Lewis Carroll.

The term 'Sun sign' means that, if you are, for example, a Gemini, the Sun was in the zone of the zodiac called Gemini when you were born, approximately between 21 May and 21 June, inclusive. You'll find that the dates covering Sun sign periods are slightly different, depending on which astrology book you read. Most astrologers don't wish to confuse the layman with the information that the Sun changes signs in the morning, afternoon or evening of a particular day. It's all very nice and neat and easy to pretend each new sign begins precisely at midnight. But it doesn't. For example, except for leap year variations, the Sun, for the last several decades as well as at the present, both leaves Aries and enters Taurus sometime on 20 April. It's important to know that 20 April contains both signs. Otherwise, you might go around all your life thinking you're a Taurus when you're really an Aries. Remember that if you were born on the *first* or the *last* day of any of the Sun sign periods, you'll have to know the exact time and the longitude and latitude of your birth to judge whether or not the Sun had changed signs by that hour.

Contents

Foreword

How to understand Sun signs

A tale begun in other days,
When summer suns were glowing –
A simple chime, that served to time
The rhythm of our rowing –

Some day, you will doubtless want the complete details of your personal natal chart. Meanwhile, you can be sure that studying your Sun sign is an important first step. However, studying your Sun sign shouldn't be confused with studying the predictions based on your Sun sign alone in magazines and newspapers. They may hit you with impressive accuracy more often than they miss, but they're far from being infallible. Only a natal chart calculated for the exact hour and minute of your birth can be completely dependable in such a specialized area.

On the other hand, don't believe the common accusation that these predictions are 'just a bunch of general phrases that can be scrambled around to fit anybody'. That's equally untrue. The predictions (indications would be a better word) apply as they are printed, to the Taurus or Pisces or Virgo person individually. They don't apply helter-skelter to any of the twelve Sun signs. They are written by competent professionals and based on mathematical calculations of the aspects formed between your natal Sun and the planets moving overhead, and they give you a fair degree of accuracy, as far as they go. The fact that they're not based on the *exact degree* of your natal

Sun, nor on the additional aspects from the other eight planets in your natal chart, plus your natal Moon, is what creates the flaw. Still, they can be interesting and helpful, if allowances are made for the discrepancies.

The Sun is the most powerful of all the stellar bodies. It colours the personality so strongly that an amazingly accurate picture can be given of the individual who was born when it was exercising its power through the known and predictable influences of a certain astrological sign. These electromagnetic vibrations (for want of a better term in the present stage of research) will continue to stamp that person with the characteristics of his Sun sign as he goes through life. The Sun isn't the only factor in analysing human behaviour and traits, but it's easily the most important single consideration.

Some astrologers feel that a book about Sun signs is a generalization comparable to lumping together all the Polish, Irish, Chinese, Negro, Italian and Jewish people – or like lumping all butchers, bakers, candlestick makers, merchants or Indian chiefs. Though I respect their feelings, I can't agree with them. True, Sun signs can be misleading if they're used with the wrong attitude. But in the absence of a natal chart, they're far ahead of any other known quick, reliable method of analysing people and learning to understand human nature.

An individual's Sun sign will be approximately eighty per cent accurate, sometimes up to ninety per cent. Isn't that far better than zero knowledge? That extra ten or twenty per cent is, of course, most important and must be considered. But if you know a person's Sun sign, you're substantially better informed than those who know nothing about him at all. There are no pitfalls in applying Sun sign knowledge when it's done with discretion. Just plant an imaginary policeman in your mind to keep warning you that you might be off by that ten or twenty per cent, and you can use them with confidence.

What is a Sun sign? A particular zone of the zodiac – Aries, Taurus, Gemini, etc. – in which the Sun was located at the moment you drew your first breath, an exact position taken from a set of tables called an ephemeris, calculated by astronomers. As printed out in the note to the reader that precedes the Table of Contents, if you were born on the *first* or the *last* day of any Sun sign period, you'll have to know your exact birth time and the longitude and latitude of your birthplace to judge whether or not the Sun had changed signs by that hour. In other words, the dates which begin and end the Sun sign periods in this or any astrology book are approximate, and this is most important to remember. These two days are called the cusps, and don't let them confuse you. Some astrologers even give them a longer period. But either way there's been entirely too much stress laid on them for the layman. No matter what you've heard, if the Sun was in Gemini when you were born, it was in Gemini, however near it may be to the cusp, and that's that. The influences which may be impressed on your personality from the sign preceding or following Gemini will never blot out your Gemini characteristics enough to turn you into a Taurus or a Cancerian. Nothing can dim the brilliance of the Sun, while it's actually in a sign, and the variations you get from being born on a cusp are never strong enough to substantially alter your basic Sun sign personality. The important thing is to establish through your birth hour that you were definitely born within the cusps. Make a small allowance for them, and then forget it.

What is a natal chart? You can think of it as a photograph of the exact position of all the planets in the sky at the moment of your birth, formed by precise mathematical calculation. In addition to the Sun and Moon (the two luminaries), there are eight planets, all of which influence your life, according to the signs they were in when you were born, their distance from each other by degrees (aspects) and their exact location.

If you were born on 9 June, you're an Gemini, of course, because the Sun was in Gemini, and about eight out of every ten Gemini traits will show in your character. However, the Moon, ruling your emotions, might have been in Aries, colouring your emotional attitudes with Arian qualities. Mercury, ruling the mind, could have been in Scorpio, so your mental processes would often be Scorpion in nature. Mars, ruling your speech and movements, among other things, could have been in Taurus, so you would speak rather slowly, like a Taurean. Venus might have been in Capricorn, giving you an essentially Capricorn attitude in love, artistic and creative matters – and so on with the other planets. Yet, none of these placements will totally erase the basic qualities of your Gemini Sun. They simply refine the details of your complex personality.

There are other factors to consider if you're to be one hundred per cent correctly analysed. For one thing, the aspects formed between the planets and the luminaries at your birth can modify their positions in the signs. But the most important consideration is your ascendant – the sign rising on the eastern horizon when you took your first breath – and its exact degree. Your ascendant greatly modifies the personal appearance (though your Sun sign has a lot to say about that, too) and it forms your true inner nature, upon which the motivations of your Sun sign are based. If your ascendant is Aquarius, for example, you may have strong Aquarian leanings, and wonder why the descriptions of your Gemini Sun sign don't include all of your idiosyncrasies and secret longings. The two most important positions in any natal chart, after the Sun sign, are the ascendant and the Moon sign.

You'll find it interesting to obtain your ascendant from an astrologer (which can be done quickly over the telephone), and then read the description for that sign, along with your regular Sun sign. You'll find that the two of them blended make up your total personality to a remarkable degree. A third blending of your Moon sign with the other two will give you an even more complete picture.

Next, the houses of the horoscope must be considered. These are mathematically computed locations in the natal chart which have influence over different areas of your life. There are twelve of them, one for each sign. The first house is always ruled by the sign on your ascendant, and so on, in counter-clockwise order around the circle which forms the horoscope. The astrologer who has carefully calculated your natal chart, based on the exact time of your birth and its geographical location, must interpret the meaning of each sign's influence on these houses – or locations – also taking into consideration the planets which fall into their specified areas. Blending all the foregoing factors in analysing your character, your potential, and the indications of your past and future mistakes and possibilities (which are based on the aspects of the progressed and transiting planets to your natal planet positions) is called the art of synthesis in astrology. That's what takes the time, talent, effort and knowledge of the astrologer. Calculating the chart itself is a relatively simple task, once certain mathematical formulas are followed.

But back to your Sun sign, because, after all, that's what this book is about. In a way, saying that you're a Gemini is rather like saying you're from New York, which isn't the generalization it seems to be. Wouldn't it be fairly easy to spot a Texan in a New York bar – or a New Yorker in a Texas restaurant? Isn't there a considerable difference between a Georgian politician and a Chicago industrialist? Of course. A rather marked difference.

Imagine that you're a Texan, discussing a man who is about to arrive for a business meeting. Someone says, 'He's a New Yorker,' and immediately an image is formed. He'll probably have faster, more clipped speech than a Texan, be less warm in his personal relationships, and will want to plunge into business without too many preliminary pleasantries. He'll probably be in a hurry to get the contracts signed and catch a plane back to the east coast. He'll be sophisticated to some degree, and probably more liberal than the Texan in his politics. Why is this instant impression likely to be pretty accurate? Because the New Yorker lives a fast life in a fast city, where slow reactions may lose him the seat on the subway or the taxi in the rain. He's constantly rubbing shoulders or elbows with the famous, so he's not easily awed. He has access to the latest plays and the best museums, so it's hard for him to remain unsophisticated. Due to higher crime rates and crowded living conditions, he won't be as hospitable or as interested in his neighbours as the Texan – his personality will be somewhat cooler.

Of course, a New Yorker can be a slow-talking Taurean or a slow-moving Capricorn, but he wouldn't be quite as slow as the Texan Taurean or Capricorn, would he? Nor would a fast-thinking and acting Gemini be quite as fast if he lived in Texas as he would if he lived in New York. It's all relative.

All right, he's a New Yorker. Now assume you discover he's Italian. Another image. He's a writer for television. A third image. He's married, with six children – and yet another dimension of the man is revealed. Therefore (although this is an analogy, and all analogies are imperfect), saying he's a New Yorker is like saying he's a Gemini, for instance, and adding the further information is comparable to knowing that his Moon was in Virgo and he had a Scorpio ascendant when he was born, etc. But even without the extra knowledge, just knowing that he's a New Yorker puts you considerably ahead of those who don't know if he's from Tibet or the South Sea Islands. In the same way, even without a natal chart, just knowing a man is a Gemini or a Leo can give you more understanding of him than could ever be possessed by those who don't know if they're coping with a fiery Sagittarius or an earthy Taurus.

It's true that a detailed nativity can infallibly reveal the finer nuances of character. It can indicate marked inclinations towards or against dope addiction, promiscuity, frigidity, homosexuality, multiple marriages, a disturbed childhood, alienation from or neurotic attachments to relatives, hidden talents, career and financial potential. It can show clearly tendencies to honesty or dishonesty, cruelty, violence, fears, phobias and psychic ability; plus many other strengths and weaknesses of inner character which may be latent for years, then burst forth under provocation during planetary progressions and transits which affect the natal planet positions for a temporary period of time. Susceptibility and immunity to accident and disease are revealed, secret attitudes towards drink, sex, work, religion, children, romance — and the list could go on and on. There are no secrets hidden from the accurately calculated natal chart. None except your own decision concerning how much of your individual free will you may decide to exercise.

However, in the absence of such a complete analysis, everyone can profit from a study of Sun signs, and the knowledge can make us more tolerant of one another. Once you understand how deeply ingrained certain attitudes are in people's natures, you'll become more sympathetic towards their behaviour. Learning Sun signs can help cool, poised Scorpio parents to be more patient with the quick brightness they would otherwise think was restless fidgeting in a Gemini child. It helps extroverted students understand introverted teachers, and vice versa. You'll forgive the Virgo his pickiness when you realize he was born to keep every hair straight and to untangle issues by examining each detail. It's easier to bear the carelessness of the Sagittarian when you understand he's too busy finding causes to cherish and defend to look where he's going every minute or notice whose toes he's stepping on. His frankness will cut less when you're aware of his compulsion to speak the truth, whatever the cost.

You won't be as hurt when a Capricorn doesn't 'ooh' and 'ah' over the gift you gave him, after you've remembered that he's deeply grateful, but incapable of showing his pleasure openly. His insistence on duty will chafe less when you know that he disciplines himself as severely as he does others. Putting up with the endless Libran arguments and hesitations is somehow more bearable with the Sun sign knowledge that he's only trying to be fair and reach an impartial decision. The Aquarian won't seem as rude when he roots into your private life if you stop to think he was created with an uncontrollable urge to investigate people's motives.

Once in a great while you may come across a Leo, for example, with, say, five or six planets in Pisces. The Piscean influences will obviously project themselves strongly, making his Sun sign harder to guess, since they'll greatly subdue his Leo qualities. But that will happen only rarely, and if you're completely familiar with all twelve Sun signs in detail, he can't disguise his true nature for ever. No matter how hard the fish tries to hide the lion, that Leo Sun sign will never be totally eclipsed – and you'll catch him unawares.

Never make the mistake of skimming the surface when you're trying to recognize Sun signs. Not all Capricorns are meek, not all Leos are outwardly domineering and not all Virgos are virgins. You'll find an occasional Aries with a savings account, a quiet Gemini or even a practical Pisces. But look beyond the one or two traits that threw you off. You'll catch that flashy Capricorn peeking at the social register – the shy Leo pouting over a slight to his vanity – and the rare flirtatious Virgo buying insecticide by the case, because it's cheaper. The quiet Gemini may not talk fast, but her mind can operate at jet speed. The exceptional thrifty Aries will wear a bright-red Mars coat to the bank or talk back to a rude bank clerk – and the practical Pisces secretly writes poetry or invites six orphans for dinner every Thanksgiving. No one can successfully hide his or her Sun sign from you, if you keep your eyes and ears open. Even your pet will show unmistakable Sun sign traits. Don't move the food dish of a Virgo cat to a strange spot – and never try to ignore a Leo dog.

It's fun to practise with famous people, politicians,

fictional heroes and heroines. Try to guess their sign, or what sign they most represent. It sharpens your astrological wits. You can even try comic-strip characters. Good old Charlie Brown is obviously a Libran, and Lucy could only be a Sagittarius with an Aries ascendant and her Moon in Virgo. As for Snoopy, well, anyone can easily see he's an Aquarian dog, the way he wears that crazy scarf and the World War I aviator's cap, while he chases an imaginary Red Baron from the roof of his dog house. (Snoopy may also have an afflicted Neptune.) Try it yourself, and you'll have lots of fun. But what's more important, as you play the Sun sign game, you'll be learning something very serious and useful: how to recognize people's hidden dreams, secret hopes and true characters – how to understand their deepest needs – how to like them better and make them like you – how to really know the people you know. It's a happier world, and people are pretty great, when you look for the rainbows hidden inside them.

Isn't that really life's major problem? Understanding? Abraham Lincoln said it simply and clearly: 'To correct the evils, great and small, which spring from positive enmity among strangers, as nations or as individuals, is one of the highest functions of civilization.'

Start right now to study your Sun signs, use reasonable caution when you apply them, and people will wonder where you got all your new perception when you begin to unmask their real natures. In fact, understanding the twelve Sun signs will literally change your life. You're on your way to understanding people you've never even met. You'll soon feel closer to strangers, as well as to friends, and isn't that really rather wonderful?

It's nice to know you . . .

Linda Goodman

'It takes all the running you can do,
to keep in the same place.
If you want to get somewhere else,
you must run at least twice as fast as that!'

GEMINI
the Twins

22 May to 21 June

How to Recognize Gemini

'I wish you wouldn't keep appearing
And vanishing so suddenly
You make one quite giddy!'
This time it vanished quite slowly,
beginning with the end of the tail,
and ending with the grin,
which remained for some time
after the rest of it had gone.

If there are times when a Gemini person makes you think you're seeing double, don't run out and change your glasses. Just remember that Gemini is the sign of the twins, and there are two distinct sides to his changeable personality. Now you see it, now you don't. Was it love you thought you caught fleetingly on those mobile features? Hate? Ecstasy? Intelligence? Idealism? Sorrow? Joy? The mercurial changes of a Gemini's expression are as fascinating to watch as the psychedelic lights in a discothèque. It's hard to tell where reality ends and illusion begins. They blend – then they separate.

Knowing where to look for this versatile creature requires a little forethought. He may be one place today and somewhere else tomorrow. Suddenly, too. A Gemini can change his clothes, his job, his love life or his residence as fast as he changes his mind, and that's pretty fast. Finding a good example to study may keep you hopping. You could try a bookshop. He's a browser, because he can get the gist of the contents in a brief scanning of the pages. (It's no accident that John F. Kennedy was a speed reader.) Mercury people also have that nasty habit of reading the last page first. If you know a Gemini who has ever read a book from beginning to end without getting bored halfway through, send him to the Smithsonian Institute, Washington, DC as a curio (or check his natal chart to see if he has Taurus, Capricorn or one of the more persistent signs on the ascendant). Geminis like to skip back and forth in a book, a pattern of action they also prefer when it comes to things other than reading.

You're sure to find a Gemini or two skimming through the halls and matching wits with people in a radio station, a public relations firm, a publishing house, a telephone answering service, an auto showroom or an advertising agency – if you can catch one between appointments. When you've found this quicksilver person, study him carefully, even if you do get exhausted following him around. The first thing you'll notice is a nervous energy that fairly snaps, crackles and pops in the air around him. If he has a Scorpio, Libra, Cancer or Capricorn moon, he may not vibrate with so much obvious crackle, but the snap and pop are latent, and you'll sense their presence under the influence of the other planetary positions. An occasional Gemini will speak slowly, but most of them talk fast. All of them listen fast.

Man or woman, Gemini is impatient with conservative stick-in-the-muds, or with people who can't make up their minds where they stand on particular issues. Gemini knows where he stands, at least for the moment.

Unless there's a conflicting ascendant, the Gemini build is generally slender, agile and taller than average. Many of them have small, sharp features, as if they were cut in a cameo. You'll find some with brown eyes, of course, but the majority of those ruled by Mercury will have beautiful crystal-clear hazel, blue, green or grey eyes, that twinkle and dart here and there. Geminis never rest their eyes on one object for more than a few seconds. In fact, their alert, quick-moving eyes are often the easiest way to recognize them. The complexion tends to be rather pale, yet they usually tan easily, and that's the way to spot them in the summer. (In the winter, they often have wind burns from swooping down a ski slope.)

There's an eagerness about Geminis, an immediate, sympathetic friendliness, and unusually quick, but graceful movements. The hair can be light or dark or both – like, streaked; Twins, remember? The nose is likely to be long and straight or dainty – in either case, probably well formed. There's frequently a receding hairline in the men (from all that activity in the brain, perhaps), and both sexes normally have rather high foreheads.

It's usually a mistake to try to pin Geminis down to either one place or one idea. It's always a mistake to challenge them to a battle of wits, because they can talk themselves in and out of situations with the greatest ease. They think fast on their feet (or in any other position); they can be sharply satirical, and they're more clever than almost anybody. Some Mercury people take a mischievous delight in disconcerting slower minds with their lightning-fast mental processes. How would you like to get into an argument with Gemini Bob Hope?

A June person will sometimes appear to alight near you, like an inquisitive bird, survey the scene with excited curiosity, then dart off in a different direction almost before you can say hello. I often join a Gemini friend in Lindy's for cheesecake and some casual conversation. He's thirty-five to forty years old, but he looks like a college student, which is typical of Gemini's ageless appearance.

For a while we'll talk pleasantly, interrupting each other and easily bouncing from one topic to another. Then I'll search in my purse for a compact or a pencil, look up – and like some disappearing artist in a magic act, my Gemini friend has vanished into thin air, taking the bill with him. (The more unevolved types use this agility to leave you with the bill.) When he pulls one of those fast dissolves, I glance around the room anxiously, and suddenly, there he is – making a phone call or waving to me gaily as he skips out the door to who-knows-where.

This particular Gemini was recently engaged to a wonderful Aquarian girl (if anyone can cope with an elusive Gemini, it's an Aquarian), and a week before the wedding, five would get you twenty anywhere on Broadway that he would find a way to slip out of the noose – that somehow, he wouldn't make it to the church on time. But he did. Geminis can surprise you. Especially when they're in love.

One of my favourite Geminians is a Mercury woman who – typically – runs Belles Limited, a New York answering service. The play, *The Bells Are Ringing*, was based on her life. Possibly due to being glued to the telephone twenty hours a day, she's not quite as light on her feet as she was when she used to brighten Billy Rose's chorus line. You couldn't call her agile, since she seldom gets a chance to leave her switchboard, but still she gives the impression of flying around, even when she's immobile. Like most Gemini females, she has an extremely pretty, interesting face, with intelligence stamped on every feature, and her quick Mercury hands flutter in the air like lively birds. Using more charm and wit than the law allows, she cheerfully solves everyone's problems in the twinkling of one of her clear, blue eyes. I've watched this

woman find a babysitter and a pair of gerbils for a cus-
tomer, make out the grocery list, write thirty-two cheques
(one of her favourite occupations), phone a Broadway
producer on a yacht in the Caribbean, send nine tele-
grams, fold the family laundry, figure the week's working
schedule for her operators, find her husband's blue tie,
write down the directions for the shop where he could
pick up some tropical fish for their son, snap four Polaroid
pictures of the dog, open and read her monthly bills (then
absently file them in the waste-basket), help a casting
office locate an actress who speaks six languages, and give
twelve clients a wake-up call – all in the space of a little
over an hour without leaving her swivel chair. Go top
that.

The secret is in the Geminian duality. They can do two
things at once with less effort than it takes most of us to
do one. Mercury women often iron, feed the baby and
talk on the phone at the same time. Some people swear
that all Geminis were born with a phone in each hand.

Any kind of routine can make a typical Geminian feel
like a droopy bird in a cage with its wings clipped. These
people resent drudgery and monotony almost fiercely.
Usually, they aren't the most punctual souls in the world
(unless they happen to have a Virgo ascendant, in which
case they become human alarm clocks). The typical
Gemini, however, always arrives late, not because he for-
gets the time, but because something caught his interest
on the way and sidetracked him. The restless Mercurial
nature demands constant excitement and change or the
spirit becomes dejected and morose.

If you have a Mercury friend, you've probably already
experienced a common Gemini habit that can be so
annoying it can give you ulcers. He'll suggest some

activity to you, like dropping over to his apartment (it will seldom be a house – too permanent), catching an old Humphrey Bogart film with an Our Gang comedy (double feature, naturally – he doesn't play singles), driving out to a miniature golf range to practise a little putting or stopping in Jack Dempsey's for a few Bloody Marys. You're tired and you're on the way home. You thank him anyway, but ask for a rain check. The Gemini argues with you. Convincingly. He turns on those baby blues (or greens or browns) and weaves a cocoon of charm around you. He talks so fast and his smile is so persuasive that, after a while, you give in. You'll go. He has a few errands to run, so he says he'll meet you on the corner in about an hour. That you didn't expect, so you start to back out, but he turns on his technique again, and you finally agree to meet him. It's a real drag, killing the hour, and besides, your feet hurt, but you manage to do it, and you show up on the corner at the appointed time. Good old Jim is a half-hour late and a little out of breath when he gets there. Guess what? He's changed his mind. He's really beat. He's decided to call it a day, hit the sack – and make the scene tomorrow night. You don't mind, do you? Only a Gemini could avoid a sock on the jaw at that point. But he does. You forgive him, and what's really ridiculous is that you'll actually meet him the next night, like you had good sense or something. You've only yourself to blame for succumbing to the irresistible Gemini sales pitch. If you get stood up again the following evening, you have it coming. It serves you right for letting him sweet-talk you.

There's a deep-seated need in all June people to disguise their true motives. Like the Pisces they feel a compulsion to behave in a way exactly opposite to their real desires. But this amazing Gemini versatility and facility of speech make them terrific politicians, not to mention experts in the field of human relationships. A Gemini knows how to swerve you from your most stubbornly held convictions. He can twist you like a pretzel with his mental karate, get you to agree with him and love him for doing it to you. But if trouble develops, he knows instinctively just where the skeletons are buried in your closet, and he can use his fast mind and clever tongue to rattle those bones dangerously.

There's a strange thing about Geminis and writing. The Sun sign itself rules writing. Therefore, practically every Mercury man or woman can turn a clever phrase and string words together intelligently. You'll find whole slews of them writing speeches, commercials, documentaries, plays and books. But the books will be novels, textbooks, non-fiction or biographies. Very seldom will you find the Geminian writing his own life story. And it's extremely rare to find one who likes to write personal letters. The typical Gemini hates to answer correspondence. He'll procrastinate for weeks.

It may seem to be contradictory at first, but the reason is clear, when you realize the reluctance of Mercury people to be pinned down to an opinion. They hesitate to put their thoughts on paper because they instinctively know that what they believe today, they may not believe tomorrow – and they don't want to be committed in writing. Few Geminis need to be warned by their attorneys to 'Say it, don't write it.' They were born with that defence mechanism. There are an astonishing number of Gemini authors who choose to use a pseudonym – and even the average Geminian will eventually find some reason to adopt an alias, either a complete change – a different spelling – or at the very least, a nickname. The rule is so consistent, you can win a nice nest egg betting on it with all the Geminis you know.

Almost every Gemini speaks, understands or reads more than one language and French is the favourite. One way or another, the Gemini will triumph with words. He cut his teeth on the Oxford Dictionary. He can sell ice cubes to an Eskimo or dreams to a pessimist. If you happen to catch him in some dodge, he can change the subject so fast, and direct the conversation away from himself so adroitly, that the whole affair ends with you on the carpet instead of him. Sometimes the Mercury tendency to fool people can lead to dishonesty or criminal activity, but not as often as you've been led to believe. Although his talents can tempt an occasional Gemini to live in a web of lies and deception, most of them are too idealistic for a life of crime. Still it must be admitted Mercury gives them superior equipment for success in that field – and they can be brilliant con artists if they choose. With their manual dexterity, if they pick a pocket, forge a cheque or counterfeit a five-pound note, at least they're neat about it and seldom get caught.

If you come across a smooth-talking used car salesman who was born in June, and he tells you the blue Studebaker had just one former owner – a little old lady who drove it only to church every Sunday morning – you'd be wise to ask the name of the church and check with the little old lady (unless she's a Gemini, too). But seriously, unless the afflictions and planetary positions in the natal chart are marked, the majority of Geminis are honest – and some of them are even painfully honest to a fault. They seem to go from one extreme to another. Yet, they all – petty thief – con man – and upstanding citizen alike

– will be unable to resist putting a light coat of varnish on a story at times. Of course, that's not lying. That's imagination.

As promoters, all Mercury people are absolutely superb. They have no equal, not even Aries. The promotions can be strictly above board, but few people are strong enough to outlast the combination of charm and sharp intellect Gemini dishes out, and that alone may be taking unfair advantage. When a Gemini tackles a worthwhile project – to sell something mankind deeply needs and wants – the angels smile on him, and we can thank those born under this Sun sign for many great and lasting improvements which have benefited all of us. At heart, every Mercury-ruled person is a salesman, even the Gemini Jesuit priests and Protestant missionaries. Take two entirely divergent examples which prove it. Gemini John F. Kennedy sold the whole world a shining ideal – and Gemini Michael Todd sold Broadway a dream or two. Each in his own way, a Mercury child. Both the world and Broadway are notoriously jaded and hard to sell.

Geminis need to rest their busy brains with twice as much sleep as anyone else. Unfortunately, since they're so susceptible to insomnia, they rarely get enough. Nevertheless, they should try hard to achieve rest, rest and more rest, to heal those jangled nerves and renew the over-active brain cells, because nervous exhaustion is a constant threat. Lots of fresh, unpolluted air and barrels of bright sunshine are also necessities to keep them out of hospitals. A lack of any of these, plus suppression of activity – can make Geminis susceptible to accidents and infections involving the shoulders, arms, hands and fingers. The lungs may be weak, also the intestines. Problems involving the feet, back, elimination, arthritis, rheumatism and migraine headaches are always a possibility for the Mercury people who neglect their health. The odd thing is that the Gemini can suffer an emotional breakdown more easily from boredom and confinement than from over-activity.

Deep inside his searching, impatient nature, the Gemini seeks an ideal, and his chief problem is in recognizing what it is. It could be anything, since his imagination knows no boundaries. Money, fame, wealth, love and career are never quite enough. Mercury calls Gemini higher and higher – on and on – above and beyond, with a seductive promise of something always just a little better. The grass always looks greener just across the road. The sky is bluer over another ocean. The stars shine brighter in a different place. What is it he seeks? Perhaps some hidden, undiscovered continent within himself. Gemini is the mental explorer.

His eyes are sharp and his talents are multiple. He has brilliant humour, tact, diplomacy and adroitness – yet he lacks persistence and patience. He throws away the precious old too quickly for the untried new, then lives to regret the instant disposal. In spite of all the people around him, he shares his deepest emotions only with his one constant companion – his other twin self. The air is his element and his real home. He's a stranger to earth.

Gemini can charm a bird right out of its tree and give it five new songs to sing. But the restless Mercurial mind can too easily overlook the bluebird of happiness waiting wistfully year after year in his own backyard. He wears clear yellows, greens and blues, silver and grey – and his moods reflect his glittering aquamarine jewel. He has the light touch, echoed in the delicate fragrance of the lily-of-the-valley, and he has breathed the fresh promise of the greenest ferns in the deepest part of the forest. But the cold metal of Mercury divides Gemini with twin desires, until he stops – and waits – and listens – to his own heartbeat.

Famous Gemini Personalities

Arthur Conan Doyle
John Dillinger
Bob Dylan
Duke of Edinburgh
Ian Fleming
Errol Flynn
Judy Garland
Paul Gauguin

Thomas Hardy
Bob Hope
Al Jolson
John F. Kennedy
Beatrice Lillie
Marilyn Monroe
Cole Porter
Rosalind Russell

Françoise Sagan
Wallis Simpson
Michael Todd
Rudolph Valentino
Walt Whitman
Frank Lloyd Wright
Brigham Young

The Gemini Man

'I could tell you my adventures –
beginning from this morning – '

'At least I knew who I was
when I got up this morning,
but I think I must have been changed
several times since then.'

Being in love gives you a nice sense of warm security.
There's that heavenly comfort of always knowing someone
is going to be there when you need him – that you no
longer walk alone. All the doubts you knew before just
melt away. That is, unless you're having a romance with
a Mercury man, which might take the edge off that 'warm
security'. In fact, you'll adjust much better to a Gemini
if you send him out for a loaf of bread on Monday and
don't expect him back until Thursday. Never look for him
until you see him coming – and don't hang on to his coat-
tails when he wants to leave.

Once you've schooled yourself to accept his restless,
unpredictable spirit, there's a good chance of making it
work. But not if you're going to insist on 'that heavenly
comfort of always knowing someone is going to be there'.
You may probably never know for sure when this man is
going to be anywhere, and that can bring back some of
those doubts romance is supposed to melt away. It's true
that when you're in love with a Gemini you won't walk
alone. You most certainly won't. You'll have at least two
people to walk with you – and both of them will be him.

He was born under the sign of the twins, you know. In his case, they're never identical twins. The dual nature of Gemini combines two completely different personalities. You might even be involved with one of those Mercury men who are triplets or quintuplets, and if so, you have quite a crowd to keep you company, even when you're alone with him.

The typical Gemini is the favourite of every hostess. He likes people. The more the merrier. It's a rare Geminian who's not a perfectly delightful conversationalist. He has exquisite taste, he's loaded with witty remarks, and his compliments are masterpieces of warm sincerity. Usually a master of impeccable manners and social adroitness, he keeps the party moving in more ways than one.

You know those scavenger hunts, where people pair off with a list of whacky items to collect, like a hair from the head of a famous movie star and a piece of the blotter on the desk of the chief of police, and the couple which has rounded up the most items on the list gets the prize? It's the Gemini's favourite kind of party, because it combines the highest exposure to people of all kinds with the highest possible opportunity to move around from place to place – and he seeks both.

If you meet him first at a social affair where he's performing his fascinating multiple personality act, you haven't a chance. You'll be convinced he's the most exciting, interesting, intelligent man you've ever come across. No one could quarrel with that analysis. He probably is. It's no wonder you're excited and impressed. But before you let him change your name, be sure you're capable of tackling an uncertain future with a man whose whims may change with the wind, and whose goals in life may shift drastically before the honeymoon is even over. Geminian Walt Whitman once wrote the lines: 'Do I contradict myself? . . . I contain multitudes.' Whether he realized it or not, he was summing up the Mercury nature.

One day your Gemini man may call on you with a chattering monkey perched on his shoulder and suggest going to a flea circus. He'll bring you flowers, perfume, a phonograph record or a couple of books, maybe even one he wrote himself. The hours will speed by as you happily sun yourself in his cheerful disposition, laugh at his bright, clever jokes and melt under his gay, gallant charm. He'll say 'I love you' a hundred different ways, like no one else in the world could do.

The next day, he'll phone you and break a date for no earthly reason whatsoever causing you to imagine all sorts of things. Was he only joking about loving you? Is he seeing someone else? Is he in trouble? Your fears may be true. Then again, they may be false. A week later, he'll reappear, full of sarcastic remarks, moody and irritable. He'll be impatient, critical and petulant. He may criticize your shoes, your lipstick or your literary taste, and have some pretty cutting doubts about the possibility of your happiness together. Either all this, or he'll be sullen and troubled, his mind far away, distant and aloof. No use asking why, you won't get an answer that makes any sense.

If you survive that experience, a few more days will find you visiting an art gallery, theatre, museum, library or opera with your Gemini man, absolutely hypnotized by his knowledge and wide interests. He'll be unusually tender, full of fragile, butterfly dreams and imaginative hopes for tomorrow. Then he'll propose. Like that. Quick as lightning. You'll forget all the thunder and storm clouds, all the rain that fell before, say 'yes', before he changes his mind – and there you are – engaged to an enigma.

Yes, I said enigma. If you expect anything else, like a man who's stable and patient, who will gently play Darby to your Joan while life and love glide on as smoothly as a gondola down a romantic canal in Venice, you're headed in the same direction as a merry-go-round. In circles. Get off fast and never mind about grabbing the brass ring. Don't let the gay, light-hearted music seduce you into following a painted scene of constantly changing colours, with shades of dreary grey as likely to show up as sunny yellow or blissful blue. If you're an incurable romantic, seeking perfect harmony, you're in more than a little danger.

No matter what the rest of his natal chart says, if the Sun was in Gemini when he was born, this man will not remain tomorrow what he is today, nor will he have any lasting memory of yesterday. In one way or another, he will change. Granted, the changes may always be for the better and he may consistently aim higher. But the element of chance is always there. If you're a gambler, you may very well hit the jackpot with him, and find a glorious mental and emotional compatibility to celebrate on your golden wedding anniversary. But all good gamblers know the odds before they place their bet. Just be sure you do. Two rare exceptions to Geminian instability of purpose seem to be President Kennedy and England's Queen Victoria. However, keep in mind that John Kennedy had at all times a multitude of interests, which changed constantly, and Queen Victoria (who was very close to being a Taurus by planetary position) brought about a great many important changes in her country's customs. Anyway, very few of us marry kings, queens or presidents, who have been forced by circumstances to mature and settle into a set pattern.

An excellent example of Geminian duality of expression is the confession of a woman who was exposed to it. The Mercury-ruled man was a producer, and the woman was a famous, dark-haired Pisces actress. After a weekend party with friends as the guest of the Gemini on his boat, during which he was openly insulting, rude and aloof to her, by turns, the actress was dismayed and puzzled. Later, she made the remark, 'I don't know what's wrong with him. He must hate me. I've never done anything to him, yet he hardly spoke a word to me all weekend.' Ah, but don't you see, she *had* done something to him. She had made him fall in love with her. The emotion was serious enough for him to marry her soon after the incident. But how did he react to his first knowledge of a feeling of tenderness towards her? As though she were Lucretia Borgia.

Her experience probably won't keep you from leaping into a romance with a Mercury man. Still, it might soothe the wounds of a few of you girls who have been suffering from the cold actions of a Gemini who's probably helplessly in love with you and cleverly concealing it for his own, unfathomable reasons. Geminis have an unconscious urge to disguise their true intent, to fence with others verbally and cloak their motives with dual actions. In general, they seek to confuse you. Then with true Geminian inconsistency, they'll turn right around and be so direct, they'll fairly take your breath away with their frankness and bluntness.

Loving a Gemini is easy and fun, if you don't try to get too close. There's an inner core that belongs only to him, that he'll never share with another human being, even you. Keep things cool and light, and don't be overly passionate or dramatic. Don't bore him, always excite him and your Gemini romance can be very special. Don't rebel against his changeability. Change with him. Be as alert and interested in life as he is. Otherwise, the love affair could become just one of those things. He seeks a mental companion above all else. One who can match his wits, even top him now and then, because he's not an egotist. He's a realist, and he thrives on mental challenge. The last thing he wants is a doormat or a dull mouse. Let your brain show through your feminine image. It won't scare him off, as it might some men. It will spin him around in the right direction – towards you.

Geminis tend to discard old friends for new ones, but not because they're heartless. Their own personalities fluctuate and advance so relentlessly, it's only natural for them to seek those who match their interests at the time. Anywhere Gemini hangs his hat is home. There's seldom any deep, lasting attachment to old memories, places, people and things. During a long period of loneliness, he can shed some sentimental tears, but it's the loneliness that does it, rather than nostalgia for yesterday. He's gregarious, and he hates – even fears – being alone for extended periods. If you can hit him with the message that you'll be a partner who will always be around, but who won't lean on him nor expect him to lean on you, he'll probably consider signing a long-term contract. But remember those odds. Many Geminis marry more than once, although multiple marriage is more likely to occur when they wed too young than if they wait for maturity. Not every Gemini has two wives, but he'll have two of almost everything else – perhaps two cars, two apartments, two degrees, two jobs, two dreams, two pets, two razors, two hobbies, two ambitions. He likes to double up.

My good Gemini friend, Frank Blair, NBC newsman on the *Today* show, even takes his annual vacation at two separate times during the year. His hobbies? He pilots his own private plane, sails his own boat and plays a mean game of golf. (I'm not sure, but I think Frank may be one of the triplet Geminis.) He plays two musical instruments, has multiple children, multiple awards and trophies on his office wall at NBC, multiple friends, two shifts at the network (one for the *Today* programme, another for recording *Emphasis* and special shows), two electric razors in his desk and at least a dozen dreams and plans at a time, which change about every six months. He has just one wife. (He must have Cancer or Taurus ascendant.) You'll note that he's also in a typically Gemini occupation – broadcasting. Mercury rules communication and news. He certainly has the Gemini charm and manual dexterity. Frank often pours a glass of tomato juice, dictates to his secretary, phones his wife, shaves and packs his brief-case – somehow all at once. Geminis are experts at sleight of hand.

In financial matters, the duality takes over again. A Mercury man may be at first fabulously generous, then abruptly turn miserly. If you average out his twin attitudes, my guess is that the generosity would win, hands down. Gemini has little desire to accumulate either money or knowledge. In each case, he prefers to absorb it, sort it and give it back improved. He's the communicator whose function is to create ever new, original ideas and serve others through the versatility of his quick, brilliant mental processes.

Will he be faithful to you? In his fashion, yes, he will.

There are a thousand answers to that question where Mercury is concerned. He likes to converse and he likes to mix. He's also strangely attractive to women, so there may be occasions for whispers and suspicions. But you can count on this: it's a rare Gemini man whose deeply ingrained sense of fairness will let him be dishonest in his actions if you have faith in him. I mean real faith and real trust. No the kind that secretly wonders. He'll always be able to sense if you secretly wonder. Mercury minds often intercept your private thoughts as though you were broadcasting them. However, it's not a good idea to expect a Gemini husband to give all females a cold shoulder just because he wears a wedding band. Females are part of the scene, and Gemini must make the scene. If they're around, he'll talk to them – maybe even laugh with them or have a drink with them. It's only natural for Mercury to communicate, regardless of the sex of the listener. But that doesn't mean he has to romance them.

It's true that there are lots of Geminians who are just plain, outright promiscuous, yet no matter what you've heard, there's always a cause. To be mistrusted or misunderstood in any area deeply distresses a Mercury man. It frustrates and depresses him, and such an unhappy Gemini can fly here and there, seeking relief from tangled emotions. When he's free from a feeling of mental isolation, and has nothing to prove to anyone, he loses the compulsion to experiment and take flights of fancy. A woman who has perfect *mental* harmony with a Gemini need never fear emotional or physical unfaithfulness. That's so true of these men, it's almost a cut and dried rule. But he won't be chained unreasonably. To expect your Gemini not to smile back when someone smiles at him, whether it's a child or an adult, a man or a woman, is to expect the sun not to shine. His cheerful, friendly nature seeks companionship constantly. It could be the conductor on the commuter train or the waitress at the coffee shop around the corner from where he works. Don't try to stifle him. When anyone tries to confine the Gemini's spirit, he can become as elusive and as unpredictable as the wind itself.

With the youngsters, he'll be a buddy, but not a disciplinarian, and he'll teach them a lot before they even get to kindergarten. They'll probably love to confide in him, because he'll seldom be shocked or harsh in his judgement. He knows how to love without smothering. The relationship between the Gemini and his children is usually very close, but perhaps a bit loose, even though that may sound contradictory. As affectionate, exciting and lively as he is with young people, he may fail to insist that they follow routines, since he dislikes routines so much himself. There's also a tendency to criticize their behaviour one day and approve of it the next day, which can confuse them. Although he'll manage a good lecture, you'd better expect the spankings and really serious discipline to fall in your department. Gemini fathers tend to spoil their children.

His imagination may run away with him, and cause him to make an occasional statement he can't back up. You'll have to make him see the importance of keeping his word. Regardless of all his good intentions, a few of his quick, impulsive promises may be broken. If the children don't tie him down in any way, nor keep him from his multiple activities, he'll enjoy them enormously. One word of warning: although he will seldom punish the children physically, the Gemini proclivity for sudden, stinging, sarcastic speech may cause deep wounds in little hearts or create a hurt which can be remembered for a lifetime. There may also be a reluctance to show affection in the form of kisses and hugs, unless a conscious effort is made to overcome the natural Geminian coolness. Yet, I've known some Gemini parents who seem to give the warmth they can't release to adults in abundance to their children. See that the youngsters don't confine him needlessly, don't ask him to babysit unless he obviously wants to, and he'll take to fatherhood nicely, with one child or a dozen.

Jealousy is something you may never have to worry about with a Gemini husband, because possessiveness is not a typical Gemini trait. If suspicion occasionally whispers in his ear, he'll usually brush it away (unless an affliction in the natal chart indicates otherwise). Some degree of jealousy is natural in everyone, of course, but it's normally not exaggerated in a Gemini. Love is not a strictly physical relationship with this man. He hears more, sees more, and feels more through his senses than others do, and Mercury helps him record the most delicate impressions vividly. His love has such an airy, elusive quality, it may seem to lack the earthly passion of other Sun signs. But if you're not seeking a wild cave man, who will drag you into the woods by the hair, he should be a more than satisfactory lover. He'll speak of his emotions with romantic, imaginative phrases, and fill the hunger of your heart with the strange beauty of his idealism.

Remember that the typical emotional coldness of Mercury can be warmed considerably if you both hear the same music and dream the same dreams. He must experience a total blending of the mind and the spirit, before the physical passions catch up in intensity. That may seem oblique, but it's the only real road to his heart.

You'll have to get used to the word 'if'. He'll say, 'If I loved you, we could . . .' and 'If I loved you, there might be . . .' and sometimes never finish the sentence. You may have to listen with your heart and finish it for him. Blot out the word 'if'. He only uses it as a smoke screen or as a safety precaution. Harsh, critical nagging and continual emotional scenes will surely dull the edge of the fine, sensitive Gemini love. Try to squeeze a puddle of mercury in your hand. What happens? It dissolves immediately into hundreds of sparkling silver balls that quickly escape through your tightly clenched fingers. One Gemini man whose wife thought she knew him very well wrote the following lines just before he left her, and she found them among his papers after the divorce:

Into the dream you came
And across the soft carpet of my reverie you walked
With hobnail boots . . .

You'll often read or hear it said that Geminis must always have two loves at once. This Gemini duality, hinting at deception, is so frequently mentioned, it may cause unfounded anxiety. May I modify that description? A Gemini needs two loves. Not necessarily two women. That's a riddle. If you truly understand him, you'll know the answer to it.

The Gemini Woman

Though she managed to pick
plenty of beautiful rushes as the boat glided by,
there was always a more lovely one
that she couldn't reach.
'The prettiest are always farther!'
she said at last,
with a sigh at the obstinacy of the rushes
in growing so far off.

Have you always secretly thought Brigham Young had a sensational idea when he advocated several wives for one man? Do you inwardly envy the Eastern potentates with their harems? You needn't resign yourself to romantic Walter Mitty daydreams. Just marry a Gemini girl. That way, you'll be guaranteed at least two different wives, and on occasional weekends, as many as three or four.

Naturally, there's a small catch. The difference between a girl born under the sign of the twins and a harem is her apparent lack of interest in earthy passion. It's hard to get her to settle down long enough to take passion or anything else very seriously. Her mind is always travelling, and she keeps up a pretty good running commentary simultaneously. But look a little deeper. Somewhere, hidden among the several women who make up one Gemini female, is a romantic one – one who is capable of intense passion, if you can manage to make the mental, spiritual and physical blending complete. How to develop her, and still enjoy all the other women bottled up inside the Geminian personality may create a problem. I can tell you that one Gemini girl equals several women. But I'm afraid it's up to you to delve into the advanced algebra of sorting them out. Each individual case is different.

Her age will be an important clue to what you can expect, because until she matures, romance is only a game to her. She can be fickle and unpredictable to an incredible degree. First she'll be ecstatically carried away by your smile and your voice, even the way you walk. Then she'll reverse her ecstasy and criticize everything from your socks to your haircut, and she usually does it with such clever, sharp sarcasm, you need iodine for your wounds. Now, don't let this put you out of the market for a Gemini woman. Remember you're getting at least two for one, and that's indisputably a bargain.

Mercury females aren't as heartless as they seem to be at times. Their active imaginations create many fantasies. Romance is the easiest way they can express them, and Geminis have at least twice as much to express as other women. A Gemini man can be a producer, a singer, a sailor, a lawyer, an actor, a salesman and the chairman of a few boards of directors all at once – and express himself *ad infinitum*. But a woman can't very well swing all that, or she would be considered a little freakish. Not that Mercury girls don't pursue careers. They do. Almost every last one of them. But under the existing conditions of society a career still doesn't offer her as many opportunities as romance to try out her myriad theories and practise her emotional gymnastics.

The Gemini girl needs your pity, not your anger. It's painfully difficult for her to really commit herself to one person at a time. While she's being impressed with a man's mental abilities and his intelligent wit, another side of her is noticing his antipathy towards the arts or his lack of response to music and poetry. When she finds someone who's appropriately creative, who's at home at the ballet or in the literary world, the duality pops up again. Right in the middle of a stroll through the museum, her other self will begin to wonder if he's practical enough to make a living or if he has enough common sense to know where he's going. I trust you're beginning to have a more sympathetic understanding of the conflicts peculiar to those born in June.

Give her credit. She'll usually manage to keep her bewilderment at her own complex character to herself, and not burden you with it. She's a lively and gay companion. Most of the time (when the mood is on the upswing), she'll sparkle with a vivacious personality, amuse you with her clever, witty remarks, and converse intelligently about almost any subject under the sun. She enjoys all the sentimental gestures of romance and has no trouble making conquests. No woman you've ever met will delight you with more imaginative ways of loving you and such appealing charm. She can flutter her lashes with delicate femininity, but she's not at all helpless when it comes to earning her own living. A Gemini woman can play the giddy party girl to perfection, flattering a helpless, trapped male right out of his mind and his bank book. But she can smoothly change into a demure and adoring housewife, from which she can quickly switch into a serious intellectual, who studies the great philosophers and talks about politics or poetry brilliantly, then suddenly turn into a bundle of raw emotion, full of nerves, tears and fears. She's certainly not stuffy or monotonous.

If you think this is an exaggeration, remember the late Marilyn Monroe. Every man she ever knew, from Carl Sandburg to her hairdresser, saw her as a totally different person than the other men who thought they knew her, too. Place a photograph of her as the seductive love goddess next to a picture of her wearing horn-rimmed glasses, a babushka and no make-up, seriously intent on a lecture about Russian authors. Then add a third and fourth shot of her in a gingham apron, learning to bake a cheese soufflé for a husband whose athletic talents and warm, human qualities she worshipped – and walking sedately beside another husband whose intellectual abilities and literary talent she deeply respected and admired. Add two more photos. One showing her with a tear-stained face, full of longing, after losing her third baby – another shot of her in a bikini, gaily laughing with a handsome French movie star on the Riviera. These are not posed pictures. They were snapped when she wasn't even looking, let alone seeking publicity. It's a perfect example of the eye of the camera exposing all the women contained in one Gemini female, who successfully kept her multiple nature hidden behind the image she chose to project the most frequently.

Your Mercury-ruled girl longs to be 'really, truly in love', but it keeps eluding her. She yearns for motherhood, but often that eludes her, too. She finds a different perfection in each man she meets, as she restlessly searches for the one man who has all the qualities she needs for happiness.

You'll find her a great pal. The Mercury girl will go along with you on anything from scuba diving to speed racing – bicycling or badminton. She'll show an interest in all the outdoor sports, and still manage to look as soft and feminine as a powder puff, with a mind as fast as a whip. The Geminian sharp mentality will show clearly when her curiosity is excited by any new subject. Her

Mercurial mind will let her see all the intricacies of your creative ideas, and she'll probably throw in a few promotional schemes of her own. As long as you don't demand consistency from her, she'll be completely fascinating.

It's only fair to warn you that this girl can sincerely believe she's in love, and find other men attractive at the same time. Unless she's near you all the time, she can forget you quicker than a woman born under any other Sun sign. It's her nature to accept change, even seek it. Until she learns to control her devoted courtship of constant activity, neglecting to cultivate patience and stability, the Gemini female can make quite a mess of her life – and yours. Fortunately for the men in love with them, most Geminian women settle down into a deeper understanding of their own natures before it's too late.

Once you've proposed to her and she's accepted, you can pity all those men who are doomed to a life of monogamy with just one woman. You'll have several wives when you marry your Gemini.

Wife Number One will be able to adjust to anything you require of her. If you require faithfulness, she can manage that, too, providing you're interesting enough to have won her real love. I refer to that blending of mental, spiritual and physical compatibility, with the physical part added last, like the paprika, after the other two are well mixed. This wife will never sulk if you take a new job out of town. With her ingenuity, taste and sense of colour, she can make a new home look lovely with a light touch of her dainty, clever hand. Besides, she'll love the adventure, and there will be no nagging reproaches that you're gambling with future security. The excitement of new horizons interests her more. She may have a surpris-

ingly good head for business and she'll back all your
original ideas. You can count on her to go to work if you
need extra income, and she'll be pretty practical about
how to spend it. Although she may give an outward
impression of flightiness, she's not as flighty as she
appears. She's a thinker, and a very clever one, under-
neath all the bright, small talk.

Wife Number Two will be moody. You might just as
well expect it. She'll have her satirical moments when she
can be cynical and flippant, by turns. At the same time,
she'll challenge you mentally. But a man needs to be
stimulated, doesn't he? Go ahead, top her in an intellectual argument. (It's what she secretly wants anyway.)
This wife won't be easily shocked by life or have any
preconceived prejudices. She may decide to march in a
protest parade or join a sit-in and forget to come home
until midnight. What if you do have to join the fellows
while she's out making a speech or going to night school
to pick up a few extra credits? At least she probably won't
hound you with suspicious questions about who you were
with, where you were, and what you were doing. Don't
question her, either. You're on the honour system. So is
she. This one is a highly independent individualist.

Wife Number Three will be bored and depressed with
housekeeping routines. The beds will be unmade and the
dishes will stand in the sink, while she daydreams, reads
or writes the outline for a play. She may serve you a can
of beans for dinner without even bothering to open the
can. But you can have the most soul-satisfying conver-
sations with her into the wee, small hours. She'll sympathize with your frustrations at the way life has treated you.
She'll satisfy both your emotional and intellectual crav-
ings, be curious about your opinion of Buddhism and

excited about your attempts to write a song. In short, she's pretty good company. She'll be very affectionate, too, since you haven't bugged her about dusting and baking and all that nonsense. This wife may make a mess of the chequebook now and then. But if you suggest a sudden camping trip or a few days in Las Vegas, she'll enthusiastically pack her suitcase without a bunch of silly objections, like how it's going to affect the budget or who will feed the Siamese cat and what if the bathtub leaks while you're gone.

Wife Number Four will be a gay and laughing mother. She won't let the children restrict her, because she'll probably have too many projects going constantly to smother them with overprotectiveness. They'll imitate her independence and benefit by it. If anyone asks her how much time she spends with them, she'll probably answer, 'In our family, it's not a matter of how much time. It's a matter of how much love.' And she'll be right. The children may not always obey her, because she's inclined to be emphatic one day, then melt and give in the next, but the youngsters will love their long talks with her. Her imagination will match theirs, and they'll amuse each other. She'll probably be a permissive mother, but she'll worry about scholastic averages, and she'll probably insist on good grades. They won't get by without doing their homework if she can help it, although they may get by without hanging up their clothes.

Wife Number Five will be a beautiful hostess, an expert at the whole candlelight, flowers and sterling silver routine. You can bring anyone, from your boss to the Prime Minister home to dinner, and she'll be so gracious and charming, they'll never want to leave. She'll organize her life efficiently and effortlessly, dress like a fashion model

and love the theatre. You can take her to art galleries and
concerts – she'll be right at home in any kind of society.
Everyone will stare at you enviously and wonder who the
glamorous woman is who hangs on your arm so sweetly.
She'll be romantic and ultra-feminine, maybe even write
you a poem for your birthday. You'll want to buy her
velvet dressing-gowns and expensive perfumes, because
her gracious style will make you feel like a country squire.
If you mention a trip abroad, her eyes will sparkle. She's
a sophisticate.

Well, there you are. I may have missed a few girls in
your Gemini harem. Every husband in town will be green
with envy when they see you with a different woman every
day. If they ask you how you get away with it, play it
cool. Polygamy is against the law, you know.

Your Gemini woman will never take a train when she
can fly. She'll never be silent when she can speak. She'll
never turn away when she can help. And she'll never walk
when she can run. Her mind is full of so many thoughts
and her heart is full of so many hopes, she may seem to
need a computer to sort it all out. Or does she just need
someone who can run beside her and toss dreams with
her – from here to tomorrow? If you're that man, she
doesn't dare look over her shoulder to see if you're near.
Some deep, unexplained fear within her keeps her from
ever looking back. When you finally match her speed, get
her to slow down to your pace. You can do it, if you hold
her hand tightly and never let it go. Though Mercurial
north winds drive her on, secretly she may long to rest a
while more than you know. Do hurry and try to reach
her. She needs you.

The Gemini Child

'Will you walk a little faster?'
  said a whiting to a snail,
'There's a porpoise close behind us,
  and he's treading on my tail.'

If the stork just delivered a Gemini baby to your house, sharpen your roller skates and shake the cobwebs out of your brain. You'll need to be fast and alert for the next fifteen to twenty years, and you might as well start right now, while your little bundle from Mercury is still pinned down in his crib. It won't be long before he learns to walk and talk. If you're not ready to fly beside him, he may slip in and out of your fingers like a glob of air. Did you ever try to hold on to a glob of air?

The US Census Bureau figures prove that there are more multiple births during the period of Gemini, the twins, than at any other time of the year. So your June event might have been twins – or more. No? Don't be too sure. You may be able to count only ten toes and ten fingers, which adds up to one infant in most cases, but not necessarily in the case of a Gemini infant. There may have to be a change in your concept of mathematics. You'll see what I mean soon enough when he starts to crawl. It will happen a dozen times a day. You'll swear you just this second saw him with his hand inside the electric mixer in the pantry. But how could that be? There he is, all the way out on the front porch, blissfully chewing the petunias. How can he be two places at once? Remember that your offspring is ruled by Mercury. He's that

Greek god you see pictured in books with wings on his feet, wearing a bright, silver helmet. Stick a kitchen pan upside down on your Gemini baby's head for a helmet, and use your imagination for the wings sprouting out of his chubby little pink heels. See the resemblance?

I have never personally approved of those harness-like attachments they sell to mothers to strap around their toddlers when they take them out shopping. It always makes me think the woman is walking her dog. However, I would strongly advise the mother of a Gemini child to buy two or three of them, just to be on the safe side.

Your first thought might be that, if baby is going to be that active, a sturdy playpen is a must. I can see your logic, even sympathize with it, but I'm not so sure about playpens and Gemini children. Confinement in a small space can amount to cruelty with a little Geminian, whose entire nature urges him to seek, to explore, to learn. Even worse than the physical curtailment is the mental boredom of being stuck on one little blue and pink plastic rectangular pad, with the whole exciting world out there to see and enjoy. Periods of being cooped up in a playpen should be brief. Too much restriction and hampering of the Geminian freedom can lead to emotional depression he may not outgrow so easily. Remember, he's an air sign, and air must move. Make sure he has a variety of toys and plenty of bright books to look at when you must keep him fenced in.

Of course, he won't stay there long, once he's had it. Mercury rules the vocal cords, and when your little Gemini tot decides to exercise his talent in this direction, you'll wonder how all that noise could possibly come out of one small mouth. Bet you take him out of the playpen

fast. Unless you have understanding neighbours, who are
a little hard of hearing.

Gemini children often make older, more placid people
nervous with their bird-like, quick movements. Grown-
ups are always telling the little Geminian to stop fidgeting,
or to be patient and do one thing at a time. But doing
two things at a time is natural to these youngsters. What
stodgy or poised people call fidgety is, to the Gemini,
merely his normal state of activity. It's wrong to make
him feel he would get more approval if he tried to imitate
the slower, less lively people. He should be taught to slow
down a little, perhaps, for his own good, but his basic
nature can't be changed without frustrating his natural
inclinations. We should try to remember that the quick
Gemini child who annoys his more introverted elders –
and the quiet, careful Capricorn child who irritates his
more aggressive elders, are simply being themselves.
Being yourself is always hard enough to do, without
people trying to force a personality change.

Love your Gemini child for what he is – a friendly,
alert, inquisitive and precocious little person. You can't
turn the firefly into a snail or the snail into a firefly. Nor
can the leopard change his spots. I might add that, if
someone tries to scrub them off, he'll be a mighty
unhappy, neurotic leopard.

Of course, you aren't raising leopards. You're raising a
bright, interesting, enthusiastic child. But the analogy is
logical. Let those spots of duality in your Gemini young-
ster remain. Someday he may make you proud of a building he designed and a literary prize he won; and when he
manifests such a double talent, you'll wonder why you
ever tried to stamp him into a single mould. If he leaps
about as though he has jumping beans inside him he's

just practising the fast reflexes he was born with. His firefly mind can confuse you, but remember that it's pursuing a thousand fancies, sorting them, deciding which to discard and which to treasure.

Teachers will usually notice right away that these boys and girls have no trouble learning to read. Gemini almost invented words. They won't mind being called on to recite, and they may smile as the rest of the students sigh, when a theme is assigned. These youngsters delight in communicating with others and sharing their knowledge verbally or on paper. Many of them are mechanically inclined and ambidextrous. It's not unusual to find a Gemini child who writes with his left hand and draws with his right. He may bite his nails, but his fingers are normally slim and flexible, which makes him adept at magic tricks and playing musical instruments. Some day it could make him a fine surgeon, dentist or watchmaker. Gemini hands are sensitive, expressive and capable.

There's usually a marked ability to mimic others. The Gemini sense of sharp wit and satire appears early. At home or in school, the Gemini child lives in a world of make-believe and reality, constantly blending, where truth is often portrayed as fantasy, and fantasy is disguised as truth. He may give the impression of exaggerating or even telling lies. But he just can't help splashing a little colour around when he's relating an incident, and he often convinces himself it really happened that way. At such times, he should be handled gently, since he's actually stretching and exercising his vivid imagination. Rather than make him feel guilty for having an imagination, he should be told always to speak the truth and write the story down on paper. Once he masters this, he'll be able to see the difference between the dream and the fact, instead of being lost somewhere between the two worlds. Gemini youngsters who aren't allowed to express and communicate naturally may retreat into a half-world of illusion in self-defence. It's a good idea to start him on foreign languages early – which he'll probably learn effortlessly. Like the Sagittarius child, he'll find bi-lingual talents will come in handy because he'll talk a lot and travel a lot.

The Gemini child who argues with you that he can do his homework and listen to the radio at the same time, is probably telling the truth. If his grades back him up, why not? Geminis are never satisfied with one pursuit at a time. It's as if they had two lives to live in only one lifetime, so they must absorb all they can, as fast as they can. The chief dangers are a lack of patience and an unwillingness to persist until a thing is thoroughly learned. These youngsters have to be discouraged from a tendency to let their quick intellects and glib wits skim over knowledge without completely understanding it.

Your Gemini child may find it hard to be punctual, because he's always running into some new discovery on his way to anywhere. He may also find it hard to listen without interrupting, because he's caught the thought instantly and doesn't want to hear the details. He may tend to repeat himself, but he won't allow you to do so, which quite naturally may irritate people. In the classroom, he can be distracted by a fly, a piece of coloured paper or a wisp of smoke outside the window. It's never easy to get his attention, but when you do, you'll be richly rewarded by the Geminian's intent curiosity and flattering interest.

Your teenage Gemini boy will practically live on the telephone, go steady with a different person each week, change his mind a hundred times about his future career, drive the car a little too fast, putter with the engine and fix your washer. The girls will be popular and be able to turn on a shower of tears or a sunny smile like a light switch. These youngsters will keep you on your toes and keep you young.

When your Gemini child finally grows up, lots of people will tell you disapprovingly that 'he has too many fingers stuck in too many pies'. You'll smile then, and they may be annoyed. But you'll be remembering one spring day when he was seven. He stuck his fingers in your chocolate pies, his father's shaving cream, the fish bowl, the garbage can, a pot of hot soup and an electric socket. You were furious. Later, at twilight, you watched him run around chasing lightning bugs in the grass. After a while, you sighed, and asked yourself aloud, 'Why must he rush around so? Why must he get into everything? What in the world is he searching for?' He overheard you and it troubled him. You'll never forget the look in his bright, clear eyes when he answered, 'Gee, Mommy . . . I don't know. But don't you worry. I'll find it.'

The Gemini Boss

He said, 'I look for butterflies
  that sleep among the wheat
I make them into mutton pies,
  And sell them in the street.
I sell them unto men,' he said,
  'Who sail on stormy seas;
And that's the way I get my bread –
  A trifle, if you please.'

One day your Gemini boss will be a walking clock, whose camera eye records each second you take past your coffee break. On another, he won't even notice if you come back three hours late from lunch. You can try flipping a coin to predict his changes. It's about as safe as anything else. I realize that it would be a big help to know which day he's going to take what attitude.

But the Gemini executive doesn't know himself which side of the bed he's going to get out on each morning, and since he doesn't know, you can see that I can't tell you. The safest way is not to expect him to be today what he was yesterday, and cross your fingers about tomorrow.

This man can be a brilliant, though restless, executive. He's more at home in the president's chair than the other mutable signs of Virgo, Pisces or Sagittarius would be, but he's not equipped to command or lead others for his entire lifetime. A Gemini who thinks he's constituted to run a large company with calm assurance is just kidding himself (always considering the exceptions to the rule, like a Sun sign Gemini with a Leo ascendant and a Libra

Moon, for example). In the first place, it's hard for him to sit still behind a desk for more than an hour at a time. President Kennedy, one of the rare Geminis equipped to take on the burdens of leadership, solved that problem neatly. He simply released his nervous energy by making his rocking-chair fly.

Your Mercury-ruled boss must move around. Gemini is an air sign, and did you ever see air stand still? It may seem to sometimes on a hot, humid day (and so will a Gemini if you catch him in a rare moment), but that's only an illusion in both cases. The typical Gemini boss will wear a hole in the carpet pacing up and down, if he's caged up in an office too long. He's happier as a management consultant, an efficiency expert or a vice-president in charge of trouble-shooting, than when he's forced into the confining mould of a nine-to-five position, no matter how fancy the title. He deals with ideas, principles and abstractions. The humdrum and material responsibilities of the average executive eventually depress his soaring spirit. Therefore, when a Gemini parachutes himself into an executive spot, he'll be quick to exercise his acute discrimination and delegate authority to others around him. These carefully chosen specialists will really run the business, freeing his own restless mind for progressive schemes and original plans that will double the company's profit and lower its overheads. He's impatient with dull, mundane details.

If your company just hired a Gemini as your superior you can expect some changes to be made in short order. The slowest form of communication around the place will probably be cablegrams, and he may require a few more buttons on his telephone than his predecessor. Your new Gemini boss won't be on the job a week before he's inquisitively poked around into every area of the operation. As soon as he learns what's being done and how it's being done, he'll want to know why. The answer, 'We've always done it this way', will cause his bright eyes to turn to ice cubes that could freeze you at thirty paces. Gemini is not even slightly interested in or impressed with tradition. When he's told something is an old custom, that's reason enough for him to change it. The typical Mercury boss will have the furniture moved around frequently, drive his secretary into a fit of the fidgets once a week with a new idea for a filing system that will work more efficiently, and change the work schedules back and forth until he finds one that clicks with him.

There's one thing you can count on, and one of the few things you can count on consistently with a Gemini. He will never be monotonous. He'll seldom be dogmatic either. His opinions are flexible. You can't mislead him or confuse the issue, because his quicksilver mind will instantly reduce the frills, penetrate the smoke screens and expose all sides of the question with crystal clarity. That means he also exposes office intrigues with little difficulty. Sometimes you'll swear he has eyes in the back of his head – and an extra pair of ears there, too. Speaking of his anatomy and such, it's even hard to credit him with just one pair of feet, since there will be plenty of occasions when he appears to be in two places at once.

Never fear that your Gemini employer will hate you or be your enemy. Few people interest him long enough for that kind of intensity. You won't be in his thoughts for more than an hour or so at a time. That's not long enough to work up any violent feelings, for or against. Besides, he has a pretty fair understanding about how the other person feels.

It may puzzle you to discover that, although your
Gemini employer is an individualist in every way, he may
not treat you as an individualist. It seems inconsistent,
but then this is a dual sign, with more than one surprise.
I don't mean that he won't respect your individual
opinions. He will. It's just that he doesn't always see you
personally as an individual. The Geminian mind is so
abstract that he often sees only basic designs in both
objects and people. All kinds of people are fascinating to
him, but he tends to categorize them according to their
abilities, ideas and potential.

Yet this odd viewpoint doesn't make him unattractive
as a human being. Quite the contrary. Even though his
approach is far more rational than emotional, he likes
people so much they just can't help liking him back.
Without the constant challenge of human contact, he
would dry up and float away. Mercury demands that he
be gregarious and live vicariously or be miserable. You'll
rarely see him by himself. He may classify people by types
and remain detached emotionally, but he needs them
around.

Your Gemini boss will probably have considerable
powers of persuasion. He can wheedle you into or talk
you out of most anything, simply by dousing you with a
bucket of that irresistible charm and wit of his. But it's a
compensating talent he was given by the planets at birth,
that hides a basic coldness of nature. Gemini lives in
vague, airy palaces in the sky the average person can't
reach. His true character, despite his surface warmness,
is cool, aloof and lonely, in the final analysis, searching
for something inside itself more than from others, no
matter how frequently he seeks their company. Yet, he's
not unsympathetic. His manner can be gentle and

compassionate, but at the same time, he offers his sympathy and understanding the same way he offers love and friendship – from a distance.

He'll have an excellent sense of humour, and you can win him over with a joke more quickly than with tears. He's not overly sentimental, but he'll always see the ridiculous side of things. A sense of humour is a prerequisite to true intelligence, so it's not surprising to find it in the Mercury people, though sometimes it may be tinged with sharp sarcasm. There will always be a slight whirl of confusion around a Gemini-run office – and constant activity. But he won't be the one who is confused. Gemini sorts it all out and clears the muddy waters of all the gunk. His quick eye and his trigger-fast brain work in perfect synchronization. The eye will probably have a twinkle in it. He'll be the company's best salesman, make speeches and entertain a lot. And he'll probably travel so much, he may keep a suitcase ready to fly at a moment's notice. If he flirts with the pretty new secretary, better tell her he's not the least bit serious, just sharpening his charm a little.

Enjoy this boss while you can, because Geminis get suddenly bored after they've made financial or business successes, and they rush off to the next challenge long before retirement time. Before he goes, learn what you can about his strategy. It's really fantastic. He's an expert at double talk. He'll run around an argument in circles, mix you up, turn you around, then win you over to his side before you realize what's happened. Yet, as clever as he is in competitive situations, he's still an incurable dreamer, and a smashingly good storyteller. Pay no attention to what nationality he says he is. Whether he was born in Israel, Australia or Afghanistan, every single

Gemini in the world is Irish at heart. How else could he possess such a wonderful gift of blarney? Notice all those green ties he wears. What did I tell you – pure County Cork.

The Gemini Employee

'The time has come,' the Walrus said,
  'To talk of many things;
Of shoes – and ships – and sealing wax –
  Of cabbages – and kings –
And why the sea is boiling hot –
  And whether pigs have wings.'

Yet, what can one poor voice avail
Against three tongues together?

Do you have some employees around your office who talk
fast, move fast and think fast? Do they look young and
act young, forget about their ages? Are they unpredictable,
restless, original and impatient? What a smart man you
are! You've gone and hired yourself some Geminis.

It's easy to understand why. With all that charm and
guile, not to mention flashing intellect and creative
imagination, you probably couldn't help yourself. Now
that you've had a chance to watch these Mercury people
in action, you've learned that they can take an abstract
idea and reduce it to a formula better than anyone else
in the office. Your Aquarian employee can think in wildly
abstract terms, your Aries employee can toss out some
red-hot ideas, smothered in enthusiasm, and the Virgos
can organize the details meticulously. But Gemini can do
all three.

Before you fire those other people, however, remember
that the Gemini doesn't have the intense drive of the
Aries, nor the willingness to work overtime. He also lacks

the fixed and steady purpose of the Aquarian and he'll
never understand the endless, devoted dedication of the
Virgo. We won't cover the other Sun signs. You get the
general idea. Your Gemini employee is not a one-man
show, all by himself, even if he is a dual personality. He'll
come closer to it than anyone else, but you'll need the
other workers just the same.

Geminis share with Virgo, Aries, Leo and Scorpio a
built-in ability to deal with emergencies. They can meet
a crisis swiftly. The typical Gemini will make instant
decisions and go into action while most of the people
around him are still polishing their skis. He's easily bored
with routine, happiest when he's free, so don't try to chain
him down to the work bench. He'd rather do a stretch of
time in Sing-Sing than work for a clock-watcher. At least
in prison he could turn his curious mind to studying the
behaviour of the inmates. I'd sincerely like to point out
there that the Gemini behind bars is a lonely man who
couldn't find the right niche for his multiple talents in an
over-organized, conformist society. Many a Gemini forger
or petty thief is basically as honest as the judge who
sentenced him, and twice as idealistic. When Gemini is
made to feel guilty about his vivid imagination and restless
energy in childhood, then constantly criticized by the business world for being too progressive and refusing to fit
into stale patterns, his high sense of moral and mental
ethics becomes distorted, and he strikes out on the only
original path he feels is left to him.

Most Geminis are so glibly persuasive they can talk
people into buying things they couldn't possibly even use.
It's never a mistake to utilize their talents in sales or
promotional activities. When the Gemini's silver tongue
gets through extolling the virtues of your firm, you won't

even recognize it yourself, even if you're a blind egotist about your own company. Send your Gemini man out to sell the public, or to wheedle your customers and clients in restaurants and on golf courses. Or send him on the road to gather up an avalanche of goodwill and orders for business. If you must keep him in the office, be careful where you place him. He doesn't resent supervision as fiercely as Leo or Aries, but he will become nervous and inadequate if he's confined and unable to express himself. When this happens, your Gemini employee will break his shackles and breeze off to more freedom without an instant's regret. Now don't run in and take a hasty peek at his desk to see if he's still there. He won't fly away or disappear into thin air until he's had a chance to tell you his reasons and take his chances of winning you over to his point of view. Unless you hear differently, directly from him, he's probably as happy as a winged messenger from the gods could be here on earth, doing whatever it is you have him applying his agile mind to.

If there's an office pool of any kind, you may see your Leos, Aries and Sagittarius people doing lots of showy betting, but you can bet your old Brooklyn Dodgers button that it was probably masterminded by one of those streaks of lightning you employ who was born in June. The Gemini won't throw extravagant sums of money into a complicated bubble scheme as readily as Leo, the lion. He's more likely to risk his security in a situation where there's a challenge to his wits, where there's fast action and a quick return. His conversation will be full of phrases like 'Let's give it a spin', 'It's worth a flyer', and 'I'll try anything once'. And he will, too. Try anything once, that is. Twice is out. He's bored by then.

Your Gemini employee may be conspicuous by his

absence or absent-mindedness (same thing), during base-ball season or golfing play-offs. Most Mercury people enjoy these sports, and many of them have participated, thanks to the uncanny Geminian dexterity. There's little he can't do with the synchronization of his intelligence and his clever hands, and that can include calculating precisely how to swat a white ball over the fence or making a hole-in-one on the green. Sports often attract him as a way to work off all that nervous energy. In the long run, however, the Gemini prefers to exercise his wits and give his mind a workout, so he can bat plenty of home runs for your firm. Still, he should be encouraged to engage in physical activity. It will wear him out so he can sleep. All Geminis are prone to insomnia. Many Gemini employees who work in offices where they're required to be on the job early in the morning, can be recognized by the circles under their eyes.

Your Geminis will keep the office humming with busy activity, lots of jokes and gay chatter. But they'll get things done. The Mercury secretary may be the fastest typist in the crowd, and quick to catch your dictation. Normally, if she's a typical Gemini, she'll be able to form an intelligent, clearly stated letter with just a hint from you about the subject matter. In spite of her secretarial talents, you might be better off to put her out in front where she can charm the people who walk in the door and run the switchboard for you. (Doing two things at once and jug-gling them expertly is no problem for a Mercury girl.) You'll have fewer disgruntled people calling you. Not only will she sweet-talk strangers cleverly, she's not apt to scramble the cords and cut you off in the middle of a call to Kalamazoo to connect you with Katanga.

I'd better warn you not to discuss rises, bonuses,

commissions and such with a Gemini, if you can possibly help it. Use a stern Capricorn or a dogmatic Taurus or a no-nonsense Virgo as your middle man. If you don't, the Gemini may talk you into giving him a higher position with the firm than you have available without firing your wife's brother and paying twice as much money as you make yourself. He'll make it all seem perfectly logical. It's much safer to avoid financial huddles with a persuasive Gemini. If you're game, go ahead and try it. But you may come out of the huddle having promised him a weekly expense account that would support a couple of Virgos and Cancerians for a year.

You're likely to trip over a few broken hearts in the office hallways when you have Mercury employees. A flirtation or two a month and a rather fickle way of changing his mind is the average behaviour before maturity. There's a youthful air of irresponsibility about many a Gemini (unless the natal chart indicates a more stable nature). He has a mind at least a million years old, and the emotions of a teenager. He'll look like one, too.

The truth is that the Gemini, like Peter Pan, hates to grow up. And like Peter, he needs a Wendy as smart as he is to clean house for him every spring, letting him come and go as he pleases. If you're the kind of boss to play office Cupid, don't introduce him to any other kind of girl, or you may have to loan him money to pay his alimony shortly afterwards.

Do you want to make your office really swing? Put your Aries employee and your Gemini employee together in a room to discuss a new project. Then stuff some cotton in your ears to protect them from a sound like one hundred adding machines and two hundred ticker tapes all going at once. Stand close by with a big strong net to catch all the pink balloons that will be flying through the air. Gather them up, take them into your office, and study them carefully before you stick a pin in them. One of them is likely to contain a million-dollar idea.

Afterword

How many miles to Babylon?
Three-score-miles-and-ten.
Can I get there by candlelight?
Yes – and back again!
Mother Goose

Shake her snow-white feathers, tune in to her nonsensical wavelength, and old Mother Goose may show us a secret message. There may be a pearl of wisdom hidden in the apparently childish prattle of her nursery rhyme.

How many miles to Babylon? It seems to be quite a leap from the sandal-clad people of Chaldea and the jewelled, perfumed Pharaohs of Egypt to the space age – from the lost continent of Atlantis to the jet-propelled Twentieth Century. But how far is it, really? Perhaps only a dream or two.

Alone among the sciences, astrology has spanned the centuries and made the journey intact. We shouldn't be surprised that it remains with us, unchanged by time – because astrology is truth – and truth is eternal. Echoing the men and women of the earliest known civilizations, today's moderns repeat identical phrases: 'Is Venus your ruling planet?' 'I was born when the Sun was in Taurus.' 'Is your Mercury in Gemini too?' 'Wouldn't you just know he's an Aquarian?'

Astrological language is a golden cord that binds us to a dim past while it prepares us for an exciting future of planetary explorations. Breathtaking Buck Rogers advances in all fields of science are reminding us that

'there are more things in heaven and earth, Horatio, than
are dreamt of in your philosophy' (even if your name is
Sam or Fanny instead of Horatio). Dick Tracy's two-way
wrist radio is no longer a fantastic dream – it's reality –
and Moon Maid's powerful weapon has been matched by
the miracle of the laser beam, the highly concentrated
light that makes lead run like water and penetrates the
hardest substances known to man. Jules Verne and Flash
Gordon are now considered pretty groovy prophets, so
there were obviously important secrets buried in those
way-out adventures twenty thousand leagues under the
sea and many trillions of leagues above the earth.

Could it be that the science-fiction writers and cartoon-
ists have a better idea of the true distance between yesterday, today and tomorrow than the white-coated men in
their sterile, chrome laboratories? Einstein knew that time
was only relative. The poets have always been aware –
and the wise men, down through the ages. The message
is not new. Long before today's overwhelming interest
in astrology, daring men of vision like Plato, Ptolemy,
Hippocrates and Columbus respected its wisdom; and
they've been kept good company by the likes of Galileo,
Ben Franklin, Thomas Jefferson, Sir Isaac Newton and
Dr Carl Jung. You can add President John Quincy Adams
to the list; also great astronomers like Tycho Brahe,
Johannes Kepler and Dr Gustave Stromberg. And don't
forget RCA's brilliant research scientist, John Nelson,
famed mathematician, Dr Kuno Foelsch and Pulitzer
prize winner, John O'Neill. None of these men were high
school drop-outs.

In 1953, Dr Frank A. Brown, Jr, of North-western Uni-
versity, made a startling discovery while he was experi-
menting with some oysters. Science has always assumed

that oysters open and close with the cycle of the tides of their birthplace. But when Dr Brown's oysters were taken from the waters of Long Island Sound and placed in a tank of water in his Evanston, Illinois laboratory, a strange pattern emerged.

Their new home was kept at an even temperature, and the room was illuminated with a steady, dim light. For two weeks, the displaced oysters opened and closed their shells with the same rhythm as the tides of Long Island Sound – one thousand miles away. Then they suddenly snapped shut, and remained that way for several hours. Just as Dr Brown and his research team were about to consider the case of the homesick oysters closed, an odd thing happened. The shells opened wide once again. Exactly four hours after the high tide at Long Island Sound – at the precise moment when there would have been a high tide at Evanston, Illinois, if it were on the sea coast – a new cycle began. They were adapting their rhythm to the new geographical latitude and longitude. By what force? By the moon, of course. Dr Brown had to conclude that the oysters' energy cycles are ruled by the mysterious lunar signal that controls the tides.

Human energy and emotional cycles are governed by the same kind of planetary forces, in a much more complicated network of magnetic impulses from all the planets. Science recognizes the moon's power to move great bodies of water. Since man himself consists of seventy per cent water, why should he be immune to such forceful planetary pulls? The tremendous effects of magnetic gravity on orbiting astronauts as they get closer to the planets is well known. What about the proven correlation between lunar motion and women's cycles, including childbirth – and the repeated testimony of doctors and nurses in the wards

of mental hospitals, who are only too familiar with the
influence of the moon's changes on their patients? Did
you ever talk to a policeman who had to work a rough
beat on the night of a full moon? Try to find a farmer
who will sink a fence rail, slaughter a pig or plant crops
without astrological advice from his trusted *Farmer's Alma-
nac*. The movements of the moon and the planets are as
important to him as the latest farm bill controversy in
Congress.

Of all the heavenly bodies, the Moon's power is more
visible and dramatic, simply because it's the closest body
to the earth. But the Sun, Venus, Mars, Mercury, Jupiter,
Saturn, Uranus, Neptune and Pluto exercise their influences just as surely, even though from farther away. Scientists are aware that plants and animals are influenced by
cycles at regular intervals, and that the cycles are
governed through forces such as electricity in the air,
fluctuations in barometric pressure and the gravitational
field. These earthly forces are originally triggered by magnetic vibrations from outer space, where the planets live,
and from where they send forth their unseen waves.
Phases of the moon, showers of gamma rays, cosmic rays,
X-rays, undulations of the pear-shaped electromagnetic
field and other influences from extraterrestrial sources are
constantly penetrating and bombarding the atmosphere
around us. No living organism escapes it, nor do the
minerals. Nor do we.

Dr Harold S. Burr, emeritus Professor of Anatomy at
Yale's Medical School, states that a complex magnetic
field not only establishes the pattern of the human brain
at birth, but continues to regulate and control it through
life. He further states that the human central nervous
system is a superb receptor of electromagnetic energies,

the finest in nature. (We may walk with a fancier step, but we hear the same drummer as the oysters.) The ten million cells in our brains form a myriad of possible circuits through which electricity can channel.

Therefore, the mineral and chemical content and the electrical cells of our bodies and brains respond to the magnetic influence of every sunspot, eclipse and planetary movement. We are synchronized, like all other living organisms, metals and minerals, to the ceaseless ebb and flow of the universe; but we need not be imprisoned by it, because of our own free will. The soul, in other words, is superior to the power of the planets. Yet unfortunately, most of us fail to use our free will (i.e., the power of the soul), and are just about as helpless to control our destinies as Lake Michigan or an ear of corn. The purpose of the astrologer is to help us gain the knowledge of how to avoid drifting downstream – how to fight the current.

Astrology is an art as well as a science. Though lots of people would like to ignore that basic fact, it can't be overlooked. There are astrologers who tremble with anger at the mere mention of intuition in relation to astrology. They send out fiery blasts against any hint of such a correlation, and frantically insist that 'Astrology is an exact science, based on mathematics. It should never be mentioned in the same breath with intuitive powers.' I regard their opinions as sincere, but logic forces me to ask why these must be so totally separate. Should they be? Even the layman today is attempting, through books, games and parlour or laboratory testing, to determine his or her ESP potential. Why not astrologers? Are they supposed to bury their heads in the sand like ostriches concerning the development of a sixth sense, or the existence of it in some individuals?

Granted, the calculation of an astrological chart, based on mathematical data and astronomical facts, is an exact science. But medicine is also science, based on fact and research. Yet, all good doctors admit that medicine is an art as well. The intuitive diagnostician is recognized by his colleagues. Physicians will tell you that they each have, in varying degrees, a certain sensitivity, which is an invaluable aid in interpreting the provable facts of medicine. To synthesize medical theories, to interpret the results of laboratory tests in relation to the patient's individual history, is never cut and dried. It simply couldn't be done without intuitive perception on the part of the doctor. Otherwise, medicine could simply be computerized.

Music is also scientifically based – on the inflexible law of mathematics – as everyone who has ever studied chord progressions knows. Musical interludes are governed by ratios of whole numbers – a science, indisputably – it's also an art. Anyone can be taught to play *Clair de lune* or *The Warsaw Concerto* correctly but it's the sensitivity or intuitive perception of a Van Cliburn that separates him from the rest of us. The notes and chords are always the same, mathematically exact. The interpretation, however, is different – an obvious reality which has nothing to do with present definition of the word science.

Many intelligent people can study or teach astrology successfully, even brilliantly, but few are able to add the dimension of sensitive interpretation or intuitive perception that makes the science of astrology ultimately satisfying as an art. Of course, one doesn't have to be a psychic or a medium to give an accurate and helpful astrological analysis, yet any intuition on the part of the astrologer is clearly an asset to his synthesis of the natal chart. Naturally, the intuitive astrologer must also be well versed in mathematical calculation and must strictly observe the scientific fundamentals of his art. Assuming he is and does, he's using a powerful combination of both conscious and subconscious abilities, so you needn't be frightened into avoiding competent professionals who are able to make both an art and a science of their work. If anything, you'll be lucky to find one. Sensitive perception is rare in any field.

The popularity of astrology today is bringing all the quacks out of the woodwork, and there aren't as many qualified astrologers and teachers as there should be. Possibly within the next decade, astrologers will be recognized professionals, who have graduated from an 'astral science' course in a leading college. The important study of the influence of the planets on human behaviour will be then taught in the modern halls of ivy, as it was once taught in the great universities of Europe. Students will be accepted only if their natal charts reveal an ability to teach or research in astrology or to give a personal analysis; and the courses will be as tough as those in any law or medical school. The subjects of magnetic weather conditions, biology, chemistry, geology, astronomy, higher mathematics, sociology, comparative religions, philosophy and psychology will be required – as well as instruction in calculating an astrological chart and interpreting it – and graduates will proudly set up a plaque reading: 'John Smith – Astrologer, DAS' (Doctor of Astral Science).

At the present stage of research and acceptance, the safest and sanest approach to astrology by the layman is to become thoroughly acquainted with the twelve signs, which is on a par with becoming acquainted with the theories of medicine by studying first aid or sensible health rules.

Mankind will some day discover that astrology, medicine, religion, astronomy and psychiatry are all one. When they are blended, each will be whole. Until then, each will be slightly defective.

There is an area of confusion in astrology about which opinions clash. Reincarnation. There's not a person today who doesn't have either a positive or a negative approach to the law of karma. You can't avoid learning and reading about it any more than you can avoid exposure to the ouija board under the Uranus influence of this Twentieth-Century movement into the Aquarian age.

Esoteric astrologers believe, as I do, that astrology is incomplete unless properly interpreted with the law of karma as its foundation. There are others who emphatically deny this, especially in the western world, to which astrology is comparatively new. You needn't accept reincarnation to derive benefit from astrology; and the proof of the soul's existence in previous lives, however logical, has never been scientifically established (though some mighty convincing circumstantial evidence is available, including documented cases and the Bible itself). Because of its very nature, reincarnation may for ever elude absolute, tangible proof. The ancients taught that the evolved soul must reach the point of seeking the truth of karma, in order to end the cycle of rebirth. Therefore, faith in reincarnation is a gift – a reward for the soul advanced enough to search for the meaning of its existence in the universe and its karmic obligations in the present life. Proof of this deep mystery would remove the individual free will of discovery, so perhaps man must always look for the answers to reincarnation in his own heart.

But he should do so only after intelligent study of what other minds have found to be both false and true. Books written about the amazing prophet Edgar Cayce, will give the curious layman a better understanding of what it's all about, and there are many other excellent works on the market concerning reincarnation, which will help you establish for yourself whether the subject is worthy of your consideration or just so much black magic. That's the only way to approach such a personal matter as life and death – by yourself – after a thorough examination of the pros and cons.

We are heading in the direction of new respect for unseen influences, and the current interest in mental telepathy is a good example. Huge sums of money have been and are being spent by NASA in ESP tests with selected astronauts to determine the possibility of transferring mental messages through sense perception, as an emergency measure against a breakdown of present communications between earth and astronaut. Russia is rumoured to be far ahead of us in this area of research, another reason why dogmatic, materialistic thinking must go.

The excitement of distinguished scientists about experiments with these invisible wavelengths between human minds has gained the attention of the medical doctors. Medicine has long admitted that such ailments as ulcers and strep throat are brought on by mental strain, or emotional tension, and now physicians are advancing serious theories that there is a definite relationship between the personality of the patient and the growth and development of cancer. Recent articles by well-known doctors have urged the co-operation of psychiatrists in determining in advance which patients may be susceptible, so the disease can be treated early or even prevented. Yet astrology has always known that disease is triggered by the mind and emotions, and can be controlled or eliminated the same way; also that people born under certain planetary influences are either susceptible or immune to particular diseases and accidents. The knowledge medicine seeks is in the patient's carefully calculated, detailed natal chart, clearly shown by his planetary positions and aspects at birth.

The astrologer–physicians in ancient Egypt practised brain surgery with refined techniques, a fact recently proven by archaeological and anthropological discoveries. Today's progressive doctors are quietly checking the astrological sign the moon is transiting before surgery, imitating the Greek physicians of centuries ago, who followed Hippocrates' precept of: 'Touch not with metal that part of the anatomy ruled by the sign the Moon is transiting, or to which the transiting Moon is in square or opposition by aspect.' There's much that's compelling and important to say about medical astrology and its value to the physician in the cause and prevention of illness, but it's such a huge subject, it must wait for another volume.

Moving from medicine to travel, several insurance companies and airlines are secretly investigating the possible relationship between fatal plane crashes and the natal charts of the passengers and crew. So time marches on – from ancient knowledge of planetary influences – retrograding back to materialistic thinking – and forward again to truth. Down through the centuries the planets remain unchanged in their grandeur and their orbs. The stars which shone over Babylon and the stable in Bethlehem still shine as brightly over the Empire State Building and your front garden today. They perform their cycles with the same mathematical precision, and they will continue to affect each thing on earth, including man, as long as the earth exists.

Always remember that astrology is not fatalistic. The stars incline, they do not compel. Most of us are carried along in blind obedience to the influence of the planets and our electromagnetic birth patterns, as well as to our environment, our heredity and the wills of those stronger than us. We show no perception, therefore no resistance; and our horoscopes fit us like a fingerprint. We're moved like pawns on a chess-board in the game of life, even while some of us scoff at or ignore the very powers which are moving us. But anyone can rise above the afflictions of his nativity. By using free will, or the powers of the soul, anyone can dominate his moods, change his character, control his environment and the attitudes of those close to him. When we do this, we become movers in the chess game, instead of the pawns.

Do you refrain from following your star by saying, 'I just wasn't born with the strength or the ability'? You were born with more of each than Helen Keller, who called on the deep, inner power of her will to overcome being blind, deaf and dumb. She replaced these natal afflictions with fame, wealth, respect and the love of thousands, and she conquered her planetary influences.

Do constant fears keep you from seeing tomorrow? Do melancholy and pessimism colour your rainbows grey before you even reach out to touch them? Actress Patricia Neal substituted iron nerve for gloomy apprehension. She smiled at tragedy, and her grin gave her enough emotional energy to astound her doctors by literally forcing the paralysis of a near-fatal stroke to vaporize.

Do newspaper headlines have you convinced America

is doomed to oblivion in the near future, through the
stalemate of hot and cold wars, lack of national and international understanding, rising crime rates, injustice,
prejudice, moral decadence, loss of ethics and the possibility of nuclear destruction? Winston Churchill once
faced certain defeat for himself personally – and for his
country. But he put a twinkle in his eyes, a piece of
steel in his spine and a prayer in his heart. That triple
combination wrought a miracle, as the courage of one
man aroused thousands to blind optimism and stubborn
strength. The resulting magnetic vibrations melted the
lead of fear, inspired the world and made victory the
prize. He refused to be a pawn of the planets or let his
country be the pawn of their influence.

You say such people are special? But these could be
your miracles. All of them. There's enough magnetic
power in you to make you immune to the strongest planetary pulls, now or in the future. What a pity to submit so
easily and let your potential remain unrealized.

When both hate and fear are conquered, the will is then
free and capable of immense power. This is the message
of your own nativity, hidden in the silent stars. Listen
to it.

An ancient legend tells of a man who went to a wise
mystic to ask for the key to power and occult secrets. He
was taken to the edge of a clear lake, and told to kneel
down. Then the wise one disappeared, and the man was
left alone, staring down at his own reflected image in the
water.

'What I do, you can do also.' 'Ask, and you shall
receive.' 'Knock, and it shall be opened unto you.' 'Seek
the truth, and the truth shall set you free.'

'How many miles to Babylon? Three-score-miles-and-

ten. Can I get there by candlelight? Yes – and back again!'
Is it a poem, or is it a riddle? Each thing in the universe
is part of the universal law, and astrology is the basis of
that law. Out of astrology grew religion, medicine and
astronomy, not the other way round.

There's a sculptured zodiac in the temple of Thebes,
so old that its origin has never been determined. Atlantis?
Perhaps. But wherever it's from and whoever carved its
symbols, its message is eternal: you are endless galaxies
– and you have seen but one star.

Linda Goodman
Linda Goodman's Love Signs £6.99

A new approach to the human heart and personal relationships. A
compulsively readable book exploring the tensions and harmony
inherent in your associations with people born under the same sun
signs as yourself, or under the other eleven signs. Also features: in-
depth exploration of the seventy-eight sun sign patterns for both
sexes; lists of famous people under your sign; explanations of the
twelve mysteries of love.

Linda Goodman's Sun Signs £4.99

Have you ever wondered about yourself? What you are really like,
whether you'll make a good wife, mother or lover, whether other
people like you? Linda Goodman reveals the real you, your personality
and character as the stars see you, in this remarkably lively and down-
to-earth book.

Juliet Sharman-Burke
The Complete Book of Tarot £4.99

Tarot cards are like mirrors which reflect unsuspected knowledge deep in the unconscious mind. This teach-yourself-guide to reading the cards is designed to help activate and stimulate your innate sensitivity as a first step in developing intuition – the hallmark of the serious Tarot reader. Whether you want to interpret the cards for others, or use them to help gain a much deeper and more revealing understanding of yourself, you will find *The Complete Book of Tarot* both instructive and inspiring.

Robert Pelletier & Leonard Cataldo
Be Your Own Astrologer £4.99

Construct your own birth chart in under twenty minutes . . . and discover what the stars reveal!

Two professional astrologers open up the world of astrology to everyone wanting to find the key to their unique personality.

Armed only with the birthday of anyone born between 1920 and 1985 you can consult the special tables and quickly devise a simple profile of them.

Or if you want to delve deeper, here's how to draw up a more complex chart, with fascinating details on the elements, qualities and planetary aspects.

Be your own astrologer . . .

Your complete astrological guide to greater personal and professional fulfilment.

All Pan books are available at your local bookshop or newsagent, or can be ordered direct from the publisher. Indicate the number of copies required and fill in the form below.

Send to: **CS Department, Pan Books Ltd., P.O. Box 40, Basingstoke, Hants. RG21 2YT.**

or phone: 0256 469551 (Ansaphone), quoting title, author and Credit Card number.

Please enclose a remittance* to the value of the cover price plus: 60p for the first book plus 30p per copy for each additional book ordered to a maximum charge of £2.40 to cover postage and packing.

*Payment may be made in sterling by UK personal cheque, postal order, sterling draft or international money order, made payable to Pan Books Ltd.

Alternatively by Barclaycard/Access:

Card No.

Signature:

Applicable only in the UK and Republic of Ireland.

While every effort is made to keep prices low, it is sometimes necessary to increase prices at short notice. Pan Books reserve the right to show on covers and charge new retail prices which may differ from those advertised in the text or elsewhere.

NAME AND ADDRESS IN BLOCK LETTERS PLEASE:

....

Name ——————————————————————————

Address ——————————————————————————

————————————————————————————————

————————————————————————————————

————————————————————————————————

3/87